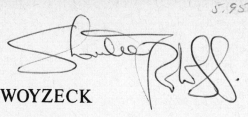

WOYZECK

Büchner, like Jarry and Strindberg, is one of the forefathers of twentieth-century theatre. *Woyzeck*, though begun in 1836, only months before its author's death at the age of 23, is often considered to be the first modern play. Its story of a soldier driven mad by jealous frenzy and acute social deprivation is told in splintered dialogue and jagged episodes which are as stunning today as they would have been a century and a half ago.

In this new translation the poet and playwright John Mackendrick has for the first time used Büchner's own manuscript, which has only recently been satisfactorily deciphered. The scenes now appear in the order originally intended by Büchner instead of that invented by editors after his death. An extensive account of this remarkable piece of literary detection as well as of the genesis and stage history of the play is given in Michael Patterson's expert introduction.

The portrait of Büchner on the front cover is reproduced by courtesy of Ullstein Verlag.

Methuen's Theatre Classics

Georg Büchner

WOYZECK

Translated by
JOHN MACKENDRICK

With an introduction by
Michael Patterson

EYRE METHUEN
LONDON

This translation first published in 1979
by Eyre Methuen Ltd,
11 New Fetter Lane, London EC4P 4EE
Translation copyright © 1979 by John Mackendrick
Introduction and chronology
copyright © 1979 by Michael Patterson
IBM set in 10 point Journal by ⩓ Tek-Art, Croydon, Surrey
Printed in Great Britain by Cox & Wyman Ltd,
Fakenham, Norfolk

ISBN 0 413 38820 4

CAUTION

Karl Georg Büchner

1813 Born on 17 October in Goddelau in the Grand Duchy of
Hesse-Darmstadt, a state of some 700,000 inhabitants.
For generations the Büchners had been barber-surgeons
and Georg's father was a doctor in the service of the
autocratic Grand Duke.

1816 Family moved to Darmstadt.

1822 Schooling, first in private school, then (from 1825)
-31 at Darmstadt Gymnasium.

1831 Studied natural science (zoology and comparative
-33 anatomy) in Strasbourg. First encounter with radical
student politics. Became secretly engaged to 'Minna'
Jaeglé, daughter of the pastor with whom he lodged.

1833 To comply with regulations, regretfully returned to Hesse
-34 to continue studies at the University of Giessen, a
mediocre institution with some 400 students and no
buildings of its own. Suffered attack of meningitis.
Helped to found revolutionary 'Society of Human Rights'
both here and later in Darmstadt.

1834 In uneasy collaboration with the liberal agitator, Pastor
Weidig, issued illegal pamphlet DER HESSISCHE
LANDBOTE (THE HESSIAN COURIER), urging the
peasants to revolt, especially against heavy taxation. August:
arrest of one of Büchner's associates. Büchner himself
denounced as author of DER HESSISCHE LANDBOTE,
but lack of evidence and his own confident assertion of
innocence delayed his arrest. Returned home to Darmstadt
and consolidated 'Society of Human Rights' there.

1835 In five weeks secretly wrote DANTONS TOD (DANTON'S
DEATH), a tragedy depicting Danton's disillusionment
with the French Revolution. March: fled to Strasbourg to
avoid arrest, and never returned to Germany or engaged in
political activities again. Continued studies (philosophy
and comparative anatomy). July: with the help of the
influential writer Gutzkow, DANTONS TOD was

published in an expurgated edition, the only work of Büchner's to be published during his life-time. Translated two plays by Victor Hugo: MARIE TUDOR and LUCRÈCE BORGIA. Worked on his unfinished novella LENZ about a Storm and Stress poet on the verge of insanity. From now on suffered frequent depressions and from the effects of overwork.

1836   Became member of the 'Société d'histoire naturelle' at Strasbourg and read his paper (in French) on the nervous system of the barbel-fish. Wrote his delicately ironical romantic comedy LEONCE UND LENA for a literary competition but submitted it too late. It was returned unread. Probably began work on WOYZECK and wrote his non-extant drama PIETRO ARETINO while still in Strasbourg. September-October: became Doctor of Philosophy at Zurich University and, after a trial lecture on the cranial nerves of fish, was appointed Lecturer in Natural Sciences (Comparative Anatomy).

1837   January: apparently on the point of completing WOYZECK. 19 February: died of typhus after 17 days' illness.

1850   First edition of Büchner's *Collected Works* in German (did not contain WOYZECK).

1875   WOZZECK first published in periodical *Mehr Licht*.

1879   First 'critical' edition of *Complete Works* (contained unreliable version of WOZZECK).

1895   Premiere of LEONCE UND LENA in a private performance.

1902   Premiere of DANTONS TOD in Berlin.

1913   Premiere of WOZZECK in Munich.

1922   Bergemann publishes critical edition of Büchner's works (title of play now recognised for first time as WOYZECK).

1923   Publication of Alban Berg's opera WOZZECK.

1925   Premiere of Berg's opera in Berlin.

1927   First translation of Büchner into English by Geoffrey Dunlop.

1967   Definitive Hamburg Edition of Büchner's works (first philologically accurate version of WOYZECK).

Introduction

By the time he died at the absurdly young age of 23 Georg Büchner had written the first truly revolutionary document in the German language *(The Hessian Courier)*, had conducted important research in the field of comparative anatomy, was the author of an outstanding historical drama *(Danton's Death)* and an amusingly ironical comedy *(Leonce and Lena)* and had created a masterpiece, *Woyzeck*, which, although a fragment, has justly been called the first work of modern theatre. Almost as remarkable as these achievements is the fact that the work of this genius remained largely unacknowledged until nearly a century after his death.

Woyzeck, for example, was not even included in the first edition of Büchner's writings in 1850, the editor, Büchner's brother, being of the opinion that the almost illegible and fragmentary manuscript was unusable. The first so-called critical edition of Büchner's works by Franzos in 1879 contained a very unsatisfactory version of *Woyzeck*, but even so it allowed Gerhart Hauptmann, the leading dramatist of German Naturalism, to recognise the quality of the work. Under his influence and later that of Frank Wedekind, *Woyzeck* finally reached the stage in 1913. Through the enthusiasm of the Expressionists and the success of Alban Berg's opera the play became better known, although it was not until Bergemann's critical edition of 1922 that the title of the play itself was correctly read for the first time (*Woyzeck* instead of *Wozzeck*), and only in 1967 was the first philologically accurate version of the text published in the Hamburg edition by Werner Lehmann. The delay in achieving this certainty about the text was largely caused by the crude methods employed by the first editor, Franzos, who treated the manuscript with acid to render its faded writing legible. It was only with the introduction of modern photographic methods that these scorched sheets could be reasonably deciphered and their probable ordering ascertained.

It is of some significance that this long process of discovery

was assisted by the supposedly antagonistic schools of
Naturalism and Expressionism, because *Woyzeck* pointed forward
towards both movements, being both realistic and poetic,
acknowledging both social causality and the tragedy of
existence. Indeed most of the critical debate surrounding
Woyzeck has been a prolonged argument between those who at
one extreme regard it as a piece of social realism, for example the
Marxist critic Georg Lukács, or at the other those who see it as a
product of pure nihilism, e.g. Robert Mühlher. The truth is that
much of the impact and quality of *Woyzeck* lies in its very
breadth of vision. As with Shakespeare, whom Büchner admired
so much, the strands of experience are intertwined, and man is
seen as both a social and a universal being.

Woyzeck is undeniably a realistic piece. As in *Danton's Death*,
which cites verbatim speeches of the French revolutionary leaders,
Büchner here uses his sources with a fidelity which approaches
what we would now term documentary theatre. The historical
Johann Christian Woyzeck was beheaded in Leipzig in 1824 for
murdering his mistress in a fit of jealous rage. The execution of a
proletarian murderer was in itself not an event of far-reaching
significance, but Woyzeck had made legal history by being
subjected to a lengthy medical examination in an attempt to
establish whether he might be reprieved on the grounds of
diminished responsibility. The investigation was conducted by
one Dr. Clarus, who published his findings in a medical journal to
which Büchner's father was a contributor. Clarus describes the life
and background of Woyzeck: born in 1780, he was an orphan by
the age of thirteen. A victim of the political upheavals of the day,
his youth was spent in a drifting existence, moving from employer
to employer in his trade of barber and wig-maker. In his mid-
twenties he became a soldier and continued his unstable career
by joining various armies (Dutch, Swedish, Mecklenburgian,
Prussian), transferring each time as a result of capture, desertion
or dismissal. While with the Swedish forces he fell in love with a
girl by the name of Wienberg and had an illegitimate child by her.
After failing to arrange a marriage because his papers were not in
order, he deserted her and the child and was plagued by remorse
for this act ever after. Returning to Leipzig in 1818, he established

a relationship with a Frau Woost, a widow of 43. Because she continued to prostitute herself with soldiers, Woyzeck frequently assaulted her in fits of jealousy. His situation became even more desperate when he failed to join the Leipzig militia, once more on account of faulty personal documents. Sustaining himself from odd-jobs and eventually begging, he went into decline, sometimes sleeping in the open, developing irrational fears and hearing mysterious voices. He finally acquired a knife and, a few days later, on learning that Frau Woost had not kept her rendezvous with him because she had gone off with a soldier, he confronted her in the street and stabbed her to death in the hallway of her lodging-house.

Many of the details of Clarus' report are used by Büchner. The relationship between the widow Woost and Woyzeck lasted about two years, and the fatal fit of jealousy was occasioned by a soldier. There are references in the report to the effect of summer heat on Woyzeck, to his fear of Freemasons derived from the tales of the travelling journeymen, to his visions of fire in the sky and to his hearing the sound of bells beneath the ground (cf. 'It's all hollow under there. — The Freemasons.' — Scene 1). Many of Büchner's scenes may have been suggested by the report: the historical Woyzeck suffered pangs of jealousy when he witnessed Frau Woost dancing with a rival at a fairground dance (Scenes 3 and 12); he was initially unable to marry the Wienberg girl because his papers were not in order (a problem that social standing and wealth would have easily set aside), and his remorse at abandoning her led to his annoyance at being called 'a good fellow' (Scene 5); he had a row with an acquaintance in a tavern after being invited by him to have a glass of schnapps (Scene 15); he had contemplated suicide by drowning (Scene 23 — although it is not certain that this was Büchner's intended conclusion). Even more striking are the very close verbal similarities between the original document and the play: Woyzeck's insult in his tavern row, 'Der Kerl pfeift dunkelblau', becomes the Drum-Major's 'Der Kerl soll dunkelblau pfeifen' ('You c'n whistle y'rself sky-blue f'r all I care' — Scene 15); the voice he heard speaking to him just after he had bought the knife, 'Stich die Frau Woostin todt!', becomes in Büchner 'stich die Zickwolfin todt' ('Stab the she-wolf, dead'

— Scene 13), although Büchner significantly uses it *before* the
acquisition of the weapon; finally, the words 'immer drauf, immer
drauf' that pound in Woyzeck's head, after he has seen Frau
Woost at the dance, re-appear as 'immer zu, immer zu' ('on and
on' — Scenes 12, 13 and 14).

Of course, Büchner also made changes in his version of the
story. The historical Woyzeck was 41 at the time of the murder,
whereas Büchner's is 30. Frau Woost was 46 at the time of her
death and regularly consorted with soldiers. Although we never
learn Marie's age, she seems as young as Woyzeck and reluctant
to have sex with the Drum-Major. Much of her relationship with
Woyzeck and the illegitimate child in fact owe more to the earlier
affair with the Wienberg girl than to that with the middle-aged
widow Woost. By these means the suffering of Büchner's
Woyzeck is intensified both by the quality of the relationship
(that with a young and attractive girl) and the unexpectedness
of its betrayal (almost certainly Marie's first infidelity). Another
change is that Woyzeck is here still a soldier, while the historical
Woyzeck had been unable to rejoin the army. The intention of
this was possibly to make his exploitation more specific and so
reinforce the social comment. On the other hand, the transfer of
the place of murder from the hallway to the woods suggests an
intensification of the natural forces operating beside the social
ones.

Some of these changes to Clarus' report may also have been
influenced by two other similar cases known to Büchner — the
murder by Daniel Schmolling of his mistress on the outskirts of
Berlin in 1817 (documented by Dr. Merzdorff in the medical
journal *Archiv für medizinische Erfahrung*, 1820); and the
murder by Johann Diess of his mistress near Darmstadt in 1830
(documented by a lawyer named Bopp in the journal *Zeitschrift
für die Staatsarzneikunde*, 1836 — the year Büchner began
writing *Woyzeck*). Indeed, since it is know that Diess' corpse was
taken to the medical faculty at Giessen for dissection, it is
possible that Büchner himself conducted an autopsy on the body.
In particular, Büchner may have derived the outdoor setting for
the murder and the return to search for the knife from the
Schmolling case and the presence of the child from the Diess case.

In Clarus' document, which clearly served as his major source, Büchner found not only the raw material for his plot but also without doubt the impulse to write his play. Clarus had done a thorough job of assembling the facts surrounding Woyzeck's case and concluded that Woyzeck was of sound mind and that any aberrations were due to his physical constitution and moral degeneration. Clarus suggested that a cure at a spa might have cleared up the former problem, while a stronger exercise of free-will might have rid him of 'unwillingness to work, gambling, drunkenness, illegitimate satisfaction of sexual desire and bad company'. This judgment, both mechanistic and moralistic as it was, would have been guaranteed to infuriate Büchner. His humanity rebelled against the glib treatment of Woyzeck as a physiological specimen, while his world-view rejected the Kantian assertion of the moral autonomy of the individual.

Indeed, the figure of Clarus contributes much to the character of the Doctor in Büchner's play: in words that recall Clarus' philosophical attitude the Doctor insists that 'Man is the ultimate expression of the individual urge to freedom' (Scene 6), and just as Clarus records how he frequently checked Woyzeck's pulse during the interrogation, so too the Doctor revels in the 'short, skipping, violent, irregular' pulse of Woyzeck as he listens to the Captain's taunts about Marie's unfaithfulness (Scene 9). Other models served to provide the Doctor with striking characteristics: Wilbrand, the Professor of Anatomy, who had taught Büchner at Giessen, used to require his son to waggle his ears for the benefit of the assembled students (cf. Scene 8), and the famous Giessen chemist, Justus Liebig, had conducted experiments on local soldiers to establish how a diet of peas would affect the composition of their urine (Scenes 6 and 8). Thus even in the most grotesque of his characters Büchner employs elements from real life. The Doctor may be a caricature, but like all the best caricatures he is well founded in reality.

Against the cold observation by the men of science Büchner sets his own humane sympathy for the unfortunate wretch Woyzeck, elevating him to the first proletarian tragic figure of world drama, and so anticipated the innovative depiction of the proletarian protagonists of Naturalist theatre. As Büchner wrote in a letter to his parents in February 1834: 'I despise nobody, least of all because of their intellect or education, because nobody can determine not to become a fool or a criminal — because if our circumstances were the same we should surely all become the same, and our circumstances lie beyond our control. Intellect is after all only a very small aspect of our spiritual being and education only an arbitrary form of it.'

This is one of Büchner's clearest denials of moral freedom. His Woyzeck is a simple being, prey to superstition and irrational fear, but with a native intelligence that makes the cleverness of the Captain and Doctor appear foolish. The servant possessed of more native wit than his master is a tradition that can be traced from Ancient Comedy through *commedia dell'arte* to P.G. Wodehouse's Jeeves, but here it is not a comic device. On the contrary, Woyzeck's understanding, which goes beyond intellect and education, is a source of anguish not amusement. As Alfred Kerr wrote: 'Woyzeck defends himself by not defending himself. By raising a terrible protest through his very powerlessness.'

To some extent he is a product of the society he inhabits. As he tells the Captain: 'If I was a gentleman and I had a hat and a watch and a big coat and all the proper words, I'd be virtuous alright'. While his poverty forces him to be a victim of exploitation in the maniacal experiments of the Doctor, the glittering earrings from the Drum-Major play a part in the seduction of Marie. Like the fairground monkey that can become a soldier by wearing a coat and carrying a sword, 'the circumstances that lie beyond our control' determine to some considerable degree the sort of person that Woyzeck is.

Büchner, himself a former political activist, is strongly aware of the social dimension of his play, but his concerns go beyond this. He is a realist but not a social realist. There is no attempt at social analysis in the play, no sustained investigation of cause and effect. The facts of Woyzeck's poverty and his exploitation by those around him are taken into account but are hardly the *cause* of the tragic outcome. Indeed, the figures of the Captain and Doctor were not apparently a part of Büchner's original conception, since they first appear in what one may assume to be the second stage of writing the play. There is also no suggestion of class struggle in the play: the dialect speech of the Drum-Major tells us that he comes from the same class as Woyzeck, and while the Doctor treats Woyzeck in an unthinkingly inhuman manner, he is much more consciously cruel to a member of his own class, when he terrifies the Captain in the street scene (Scene 9).

Even after abandoning his political activities when he went into exile, Büchner retained a strong sense of social injustice, and this is unquestionably reflected in the play. But clearly Büchner considered that while social revolution might help the Woyzecks of this world, it could hardly save them; a society however just it might be would have no answer to the perennial tragedy of human jealousy. The tragedy of social abuse is but one aspect of the tragedy of being born.

It is this insight that constitutes the other major strand of the play and establishes *Woyzeck* as a forerunner of Expressionism. Many of the stylistic elements of the piece also anticipate Expressionism. The presentation of the Doctor, the Captain, the Drum-Major, etc., as unnamed types devoid of psychology, foreshadows the Gentlemen in Black, the Cashier, the Son and all the anonymous figures of Expressionism and, beyond it, of Brecht.

The same successors owe a debt to the structure of *Woyzeck*. The episodic scenes of the play do not unravel the plot in the style of conventional dramaturgy but leap from moment to moment and are in many cases interchangeable in their sequence. Following the model of the *Stationendrama* of the Storm and Stress period, in which 'stations' of isolated action replaced a linear development, Büchner's technique anticipates Brecht's distinctions between the 'Aristotelian' theatre ('One scene leading to another; Growth') and his own Epic Theatre ('Each scene on its own; Montage'). Where the structure of traditional drama reinforced a sense of inevitability by presenting events leading inexorably from exposition to catastrophe, the episodic structure points to the arbitrary nature of events. In Brecht this contains the anti-tragic implications that the events are unnecessary and subject to change, while in Büchner the very arbitrariness cruelly reinforces the tragic sense. In *Woyzeck* we

experience the desolation of tragedy without being cushioned
from its force by the sense of inner necessity that a linear
structure would lend. That Woyzeck kills the person he most
loves is disturbing enough; that what drives him to this act is seen
only in fragmented glimpses and not as a clearly ordered
development is fearful. It is the silence that terrifies.

What causes Woyzeck to act as he does is, then, never spelt
out. What is clear is that he is not motivated primarily by social
causes. The play opens in the world of Nature, and the first
picture we have of him is of a man frightened and pursued by
natural forces. When the Doctor later rebukes him for urinating
against the wall, Woyzeck defends himself by reference to nature:
'A man might have one sort of character, one sort of make-up —
But nature's something again, you see . . .'. It is voices from the
earth that urge him to commit murder and it is in the woods
under a blood-red moon that he does the deed.

It is nature not society that is the final determinant of the
tragic outcome. There is no blame attached to Marie: however
kind and loving a person Woyzeck is, earning money for her,
gently arranging their child in its crib, he is easily outshone by the
sexually exciting Drum-Major. It is in the nature of Marie, in the
nature of the world, that she must succumb to his advances; and
she does this not joyfully but as though resigning herself to some
irresistible force: 'What's it matter anyway? It's all one.'

We understand and forgive her 'sin', but the injustice of it is
terrible. That someone so kind, so weak and so defenceless as
Woyzeck should have the last thing of value taken from him is
cruelly unfair. In words which — like the desolate fable of the
Grandmother — take us far beyond the narrow confines of the
setting of the play, Woyzeck screams his protest: 'Why don't you
blow the sun out, God? Let everything fall over itself in lewdness.
Flesh, filth, man, woman, human, animal. — They all do it in the
open day, do it on the back of a hand like flies.'

In *Woyzeck* man is shown to suffer in many ways. The
deprived individual is a victim of society, certainly; but the play
further offers the perennial tragic insight that the justice of the
world does not correspond to man's expectations of it. This
recognition, that in its depth goes beyond social realism and in its

human concern stops short of nihilism, makes *Woyzeck* a tragic masterpiece.

The Staging of Woyzeck

That *Woyzeck* is at once a realistic piece and a work that goes beyond realism presents considerable problems in terms of staging. Significantly, it was the Expressionist theatre that first made the attempt, and it is arguable that theatre practice still has not discovered a totally adequate answer to the demands of the play.

The scenes are set in real locations, but without the aid of a revolving stage it is technically impossible to present them realistically. Even if the resources are available, it would be a mistake to play them naturalistically, because their very brevity and elliptical language suggest moments in a dream rather than events reproduced from life.

The characters too present problems in terms of acting-style. Woyzeck, Marie and Andres appear real enough, but the unnamed characters like the Captain and Doctor are patently two-dimensional. Other figures seem to step out of a fairy-tale rather than belong specifically to nineteenth-century Germany: the old Grandmother, the Drum-Major, resplendent in his red uniform, and the Journeymen, those figures beloved of the German Romantics, young men that travelled from afar in their black capes and wide-brimmed hats to earn their apprenticeship. It is no easy task to achieve a unity of style that will accommodate both the realistic and the fabulous elements of the play.

The first production of *Wozzeck*, as it was then called, took place in the Munich Kammerspiele on 8 November 1913 under the direction of Eugen Kilian. It followed perforce the corrupt text of Franzos, including a scene in which the children danced round Marie's child, shouting at him: 'Your mother is dead!', and ending with a brief scene of an autopsy, employing the isolated fragment: 'A good murder, a real murder, a nice murder, as nice as you could wish. We haven't had such a nice one for a long time.' A contemporary review expressed surprise that the play worked as a total tragic experience without one's being aware of the fragmentary nature of the original and recorded that it exerted a tremendous power over the audience: in the scenes with the

Captain and Doctor 'behind the laughter irresistibly provoked by the surface comedy one trembles with tragic pity for the tortured creature and with holy anger against his well-fed torturers . . .'

The first performance in Berlin on 1 December 1913, directed by a leading Expressionist, Victor Barnowsky, was far less successful, falling into the trap of dressing the sets elaborately. The result was a frustrating experience, since the audience spent almost as long looking at the closed curtain between the scenes as watching the action itself.

Eight years later in Berlin, at the Deutsches Theater, Max Reinhardt was persuaded to stage *Woyzeck*, and the production which opened on 5 April 1921 became the most celebrated ᶜ staging of the inter-war years. Predictably for Reinhardt the social comment was played down, and the resultant lack of realism allowed him both to pace the play fluently and to concentrate on the state of Woyzeck's 'soul'. The critic Siegfried Jacobsohn remarked: 'The lighting, which is handled with great virtuosity, replaces the scenery and extends the director's art of illuminating the souls of the characters. For him suffering man is a subject of immediate concern in itself and not a means to demagogic ends.'

In 1925 Alban Berg's opera *Wozzeck* was first performed in Berlin. Based on Franzos' version, it ended with Marie's child alone on stage, playing on his hobby-horse, unaware that his mother is dead.

Apart from this operatic version which has retained its popularity, there was a further adaptation by Franz Csokor, which was performed with success in Innsbruck (1926) and Vienna (1928). Csokor, in supplying an ending for the play, added four wordy scenes and expanded Büchner's own later scenes. Thus the murder scene is amplified by providing links in the dialogue between elements of the scene, e.g. between the moon and the knife. In the place of associative images Csokor introduces literalness; he is explicit where Büchner's terse language is implicit.

Csokor's additional scenes continue in the same vein: after Marie's murder and Woyzeck's suicide there is an inquest conducted by a grotesquely caricatured judge. For their autopsy the corpses are laid out in the morgue. The Grandmother holds up the child to the window to look in at the bodies of its parents, the Drum-Major comes to retrieve his earrings from Marie's corpse and her neighbour Margaret drags him off in nymphomaniac lust. The Doctor carries out the autopsy and the play ends with the Captain being shaved by Andres, who in his dumb insubordination promises a revolt by the working-classes against their cruelly exploitative masters. Csokor's ending, which throws the weight heavily into the scales of a primarily social interpretation, has the quality of a pastiche. For all the reticence of his final scene, Csokor has not learnt from Büchner the value of silence.

In the Third Reich there was understandably no possibility of staging *Woyzeck*. While *Danton's Death* could be perverted to the Nazi ideology by suggesting that the solution to Danton's nihilistic disillusionment with revolution lay in the delirium of Fascism, the uncompromisingly socialist implications of *Woyzeck* were anathema to the Nazis.

It was understandable too that the first realisation of *Woyzeck* after the Second World War should emphasise the anti-militaristic elements in the play. This was the film of *Wozzeck* directed by Dr Georg Klaren in 1947. Made on the tiniest of budgets with film footage begged off the occupying forces in Germany, it opens with an autopsy on Woyzeck's body and the rest of the action is in flash-back. To make its point, it includes scenes in the barracks with the common soldiers, Woyzeck and Andres amongst them, having to submit to inhuman military discipline.

In the post-war years, over a century after the death of the author, the fame of *Woyzeck* has spread across the world. Published translations exist in French, English, Czech, Danish, Spanish, Italian, Polish, Slovak and Turkish, but the play is known in many more countries besides.

The most important stage production of *Woyzeck* of the early post-war years was directed by Oscar Fritz Schuh in Berlin in 1953, with Caspar Neher, Brecht's foremost designer, responsible for the décor. This production, which was characterised by its cool style blending realistic acting with an austerity of décor, was brought to London in 1957 and caused a stir which might have been yet greater had it not lived in the shadow of the visit of the Berliner Ensemble the year before.

Nevertheless the reviewer of the *Daily Express* enthused: 'I found the performance as exciting as though I had seen *Macbeth* for the first time.'

Other major productions in Germany have been by Hans Schweikart in Munich (1952), by Hans Lietzau in Munich (1965), performed with resounding success in New York the following year, a film version by Rudolf Noelte (1967), and Niels-Peter Rudolph's austere production in Hamburg (1970). It is now regularly performed in the theatres of West Germany.

From East Germany in 1970 came an interesting version by the Berliner Ensemble under the direction of Helmut Nitzschke, with Ekkehard Schall, the leading Brechtian actor, playing Woyzeck. Not unexpectedly this production emphasised the social comment of the play and opened with the scene of the Doctor lecturing his students, during which Woyzeck runs on just in time to catch the unfortunate cat thrown from an upper window — an act of humanity amidst a violently structured society. Using almost all Büchner's extant material for the play, this version extended the text to 29 scenes, deliberately sacrificing poetic intensity for epic breadth. It ended with the Doctor conducting an autopsy on Marie's body, the assembled students once more scribbling notes as the self-satisfied bourgeois academic pronounced: 'A good murder, a real murder . . .'.

Two further experimental stagings are of interest: in 1969 at the Recklinghausen Festival Willi Schmidt took up an ingenious idea that had been tried out some years previously by Gerald Szyszkowicz in Wilhelmshaven, namely to play *Woyzeck* and *Leonce and Lena* together, intercalating the scenes of one play with that of the other. The same actor played both Woyzeck and Leonce, and the final scenes of both plays were performed simultaneously, Leonce's and Valerio's final duologue intercut with the Policeman's words: 'A good murder, a real murder . . . ' Ingenious as the idea was, the total effect seems to have offered little more illumination than would the interspersing of scenes from *Macbeth* with *Twelfth Night*.

Two years later in Baden-Baden the Büchner scholar Günther Penzoldt staged *The Case of Woyzeck* as a prelude to *Woyzeck* itself (later revived in Saarbrücken in 1977). This consisted of a dramatisation of the historical Woyzeck's trial, based mainly on Clarus' report, and merely reaffirmed the old paradox that the characters of Büchner's creative imagination are more real than any historically accurate reproductions can hope to be.

The most outstanding production outside Germany was that by Ingmar Bergman in Stockholm in 1969. It was played in the round, and sought to establish a general relevance to modern Sweden by dressing the characters in costume that did not relate to any specific period and by allowing them to speak a standard Swedish that was not identified with any specific region. Interestingly enough, this version also ended with an autopsy.

In Britain there have been three particularly interesting versions of *Woyzeck* in recent years. The first was a television adaptation, *The Death of a Private* by Robert Muller, broadcast by the BBC on 13 December 1967 (Production: Irene Schubik; direction: James Ferman). Muller decided to transfer the action to contemporary England: Woyzeck became Private Watts (played by Dudley Sutton), the Drum-Major became a pop-star, and the Doctor's diet of peas became a diet of bananas. Pressing this masterpiece into ill-fitting modern dress weakened its power and paradoxically made it less truly relevant to modern Britain than the original. As Francis King observed the following week in *The Listener*, it stood in the same relationship to Büchner's play 'as *Mourning Becomes Electra* to the *Oresteia*'.

Another version was an adaptation by Charles Marowitz, first performed at the Open Space, London, on 13 February 1973. The text is freely translated by Marowitz himself in a way that suggests that he is more concerned to provide his characters with a punchy colloquial style than to reproduce the poetic rhythms of Büchner's language. His adaptation develops both the social and existential themes of the play. On the one hand, he adds entirely new material, giving the play the framework of a trial and including scenes in which a soldier passes on a revolutionary pamphlet (for which he is brutally executed) and in which the Captain tells the Doctor about his fears of an impending revolution. On the other hand, the staging of the play, with characters appearing from nowhere and with strange identifications between roles (Woyzeck playing the Showman's monkey, the Drum-Major playing the Jewish knife-seller), has all the quality of a dream. Momentarily arresting as this adventurous presentation undoubtedly was, it was a juxtaposition rather than a synthesis of two theatrical styles, and Marowitz himself admitted that he had created 'a style that shuttled between televisual naturalism and an extravagant theatricality'. Moreover, by having Woyzeck play the Showman's animals and by ending the play with the testimonies of the characters, Marowitz unnecessarily spells out connections and meanings that are already implicit in the original.

The third experimental staging of *Woyzeck* was by the Pip Simmons group in Cardiff in December 1977. 'Constructed upon an imagination of extraordinary breadth' *(Plays and Players)*, the production moved the action from location to location: different rooms of the former school where it was performed were transformed into a barber's shop, a fairground booth, a laboratory, a barracks room, and so on. The murder took place out of doors on a catwalk over a skull-shaped lake, illumined by flames burning on the water. The audience was led from one scene to the next by the motley collection of grotesquely attired performers, until they were brought finally to the foot of the guillotine on which Woyzeck was to be executed.

Although all three of these British productions of *Woyzeck* were adventurous and interesting, it is a pity that the British theatre is not better acquainted with the play that Büchner wrote. It may be rewarding to update Shakespeare, to play games with his text or to stage his plays environmentally, but then we are familiar with the original. But no such familiarity exists with *Woyzeck,* and it is fair to make a plea that the mildly xenophobic British theatre should take a closer look at a play of such modernity and such excellence.

There has indeed been one 'straight' production of *Woyzeck* to which large sections of the British public have had access, namely the Open University television adaptation of the play, directed by John Selwyn Gilbert. The translation used was that by Victor Price, containing as it does some inaccuracies and dubious contamination (see below), but at least the ordering of the scenes took into account the researches of Lehmann. The conclusion was open-ended, employing the second scene of the H3 manuscript (Woyzeck. Child. Fool) as the final scene.

The television medium did not always serve the piece well. For example, the essential contrast in the first scene between Woyzeck's nervous anguish and Andres' matter-of-fact composure was lost by concentrating on close-ups of Woyzeck's tormented face. Frequently, too, the actors over-projected, injecting emotion into lines that can be trusted to do their own work without pursuing unconvincing intensity. There was also some curious doubling: the Journeymen of the Tavern, played by grotesque ancients with beards, reappeared as the students at the Doctor's lecture, and the Showman was identical with the Fool. While there was some suggestion of Expressionistic setting, as in the *Dr. Caligari*-like distorted angles of the Street scenes, totally Naturalistic sound-effects were used.

Apart from the somewhat gratuitous close-up view of Marie being brought to orgasm by the Drum-Major in the street, there was little tampering with the original, and one may be grateful for an adequate if unspectacular version of Büchner's work. Nevertheless, the British theatre still awaits a production worthy of the text, and one can but hope that this new translation will encourage a director of imagination to attempt its realisation.

The Variant Texts
Thanks to the researches of Lehmann (1967) and Krause (1969) we are at last in possession of as philologically accurate a text of *Woyzeck* as we can now hope for. There are extant four basic stages in the composition of *Woyzeck*: the so-called H1 manuscript, which deals with Marie's infidelity and the murder by Woyzeck (here called Louis); the H2 draft, which sketches in more fully Woyzeck's background and introduces for the first time the figures of the Captain and the Doctor; H3, which consists of two isolated scenes (the Doctor lecturing to his students and Woyzeck with his child and the Fool); and finally H4, which draws together most of the scenes of the earlier drafts, paring down some of the dialogue, adding some entirely new material (e.g. Woyzeck shaving the Captain, the seduction of

Marie, the purchase of the knife and Woyzeck's bequeathing of his possessions), and breaking off before the murder. Since this last draft, unlike the earlier three, was in a reasonably legible hand and since it is almost certain from Büchner's last letter to his fiancée that he intended to complete *Woyzeck* within eight days, it is fair to assume that this H4 manuscript is, up to the point where it breaks off, an authentic record of Büchner's intentions with regard to the final version of the text.

These findings affect two problems regarding the preparation of the text for the stage: first, the ordering of the scenes, and secondly the question of contamination, that is to say, how much of Büchner's earlier drafts should be used in structuring a final version.

The first problem is more easily solved. One merely has to follow the order of scenes as given in H4 and, where it breaks off, follow — for want of any later material — the order of scenes in H1.

This still leaves open the question of how the play should end, because H1 seems to offer two possible conclusions. The penultimate two scenes show Louis/Woyzeck returning to the scene of the crime to dispose of the murder weapon in a pond, while in the last fragmentary scene there is a court-usher commenting with satisfaction on the 'good murder' in the presence of a barber, a doctor and a judge. The scene also contains what appears to be brief notes on the figure of the Barber.

This ambiguous evidence suggests that Büchner intended the play to end either with Woyzeck's drowning in the pond or with his trial. The evidence for the latter possibility, which would tend to place further emphasis on the social concerns of the play, are as follows:

(i) The historical model Woyzeck was put on trial and executed;

(ii) Büchner's own concern with the question of Woyzeck's responsibility for his crime, which might best have been examined in a trial-scene;

(iii) In trying to conceal the evidence by disposing of the knife, Woyzeck seems intent on avoiding arrest rather than to be contemplating suicide;

(iv) The last scene of H1 prescribes the presence of the 'Barber' in what appears to be a court.

In reply to these points it may be argued:

(i) Büchner showed himself in no way bound by his historical model and used the facts only where they suited him;

(ii) The play itself stands as the best examination of Woyzeck's responsibility, and any court debate would be superfluous and anti-climactic;

(iii) Such contradictory behaviour would not be untypical for a murderer in a confused state of mind before his imminent demise, and the drowning may anyway be accidental rather than suicidal;

(iv) It is unlikely that the Barber of the final scene of H1 is Woyzeck. The historical Woyzeck was a barber, but there is nothing in H1 to suggest that he is anything other than a soldier (the odd-jobs like shaving the Captain are introduced in H2). In H1 Woyzeck is consistently referred to as Louis, and the Barber's speeches in an earlier scene are quite different from those spoken by Louis/Woyzeck. The notes on the Barber suggest a certain physical resemblance to Woyzeck ('tall, thin') but he is called a 'dogmatic atheist', which is a totally inappropriate designation for Woyzeck. Perhaps Büchner originally intended to call upon the Barber to provide a detached commentary at what would seem to be an inquest rather than a trial.

There is little evidence that Büchner intended his Woyzeck to be brought to trial, and in the many stage adaptations I have encountered almost none provide this particular ending. The exceptions are the Penzoldt dramatisation of the trial, which is a documentary addition rather than an attempt to provide an ending to the original, and the adaptations by Charles Marowitz and Pip Simmons.

The evidence that Büchner intended Woyzeck to drown is provided by the following:

(i) The historical Woyzeck heard voices urging him to 'jump into the water';

(ii) Woyzeck's death would provide a much more climactic ending and a greater sense of loss;

(iii) On a practical level, if Büchner intended to complete the play within eight days, it is hard to conceive that he could have been contemplating what would have amounted to an entirely new ending;

(iv) The scene in H1, in which he goes further and further into the pond, suggests, if it is complete, the only possible conclusion that he will continue into ever deeper water;

(v) In the scene in the barracks with Andres where he is disposing of his belongings, Woyzeck seems to be taking leave of this life.

In reply to these points it might be asserted:

(i) Again, Büchner is not bound by historical fact, and while he used other voices in the play, he did not use this particular one;

(ii) This depends on the circular argument that because the play breaks off where it does, it has a tragic quality, and that to maintain the tragic quality, it cannot continue effectively after this point;

(iii) Perhaps he had in mind only a very brief trial scene more in the nature of a summing up than a debate;

(iv) To counter this, there is in H3 the brief scene in which the Fool calls to Woyzeck: 'This one fell in the water.' But it is by no means clear where Büchner intended to place this scene, and the phrase in German is anyway part of a counting-rhyme (like 'This little piggy went to market') and would be a crude device if used here literally. It seems unlikely that it was intended to be placed after Woyzeck's return from the pond.

(v) It is not inconceivable, though less likely, that Woyzeck should behave like this in preparation for his almost certain arrest rather than for his death.

We can never know how *Woyzeck* was meant to end, but in balance I believe the evidence points towards Woyzeck's drowning. This is not to say, as is so often asserted, that Woyzeck necessarily commits suicide. There is a whole area between death by misadventure and a deliberate decision to take one's life into which Woyzeck's drowning may fall. Simply to call this suicide is to limit unnecessarily the possibilities of the ending.

Culminating in the penultimate scene of H1, Woyzeck going into the water, the most likely ordering of the scenes is as follows:

1. Woyzeck and Andres cutting sticks.
2. Marie sees Drum-Major; Woyzeck on his way to muster.
3. Fairground.
4. Marie with earrings.
5. Woyzeck shaving Captain.
6. Marie succumbs to Drum-major.
7. Woyzeck confronts Marie.
8. Doctor reproaches Woyzeck for urinating on wall.
9. Doctor and Captain in the street.
10. Woyzeck leaves Andres to go off to dance.
11. Woyzeck sees Marie and Drum-Major dancing in tavern.
12. Woyzeck hears voice: 'Stab the she-wolf, dead.'
13. Woyzeck tries to tell Andres of the voices.
14. Drum-Major fights Woyzeck in tavern.
15. Woyzeck buys knife.
16. Marie reading Bible.
17. Woyzeck bequeathing his belongings.
18. Grandmother's fable; Woyzeck fetches Marie.
19. Woyzeck kills Marie.
20. Passers-by hear cries.
21. Woyzeck returns to tavern.
22. Children rush off to see Marie's body.
23. Woyzeck returns to body to retrieve knife.
24. Woyzeck throws knife into pond.

In addition to these 24 scenes there remains the possibility that Büchner intended also to use one or both of the scenes of H3. The first of these, the Doctor lecturing to his students, is possibly one of the first scenes Büchner composed, since the Doctor is called Professor until half-way through the scene. It was not taken up into Büchner's fair-copy and it would destroy the momentum of the scenes if one were to place it after Scene 17, where the fair-copy breaks off. The other scene, in which Woyzeck is rejected by his child, could be placed among these later scenes, and some critics have even suggested ending the play with it. It would be much more meaningful and poignant, though, if Woyzeck were to encounter the child being looked after by the Fool and be rejected by it, while Marie was off with her Drum-Major. A possible placing might be just before or just after Scene 11 (the tavern), but since Büchner did not incorporate either of these scenes in the H4 fair-copy, it is probable that he did not intend to use them.

From this revised ordering of scenes some interesting points emerge. Perhaps most striking is the fact that the play does not open with Woyzeck shaving the Captain. The scene was placed there by an earlier editor on the unsatisfactory grounds that it contained more exposition than any other scene, thus confusing Büchner's advanced dramaturgy with a more conventional dramatic style. By restoring this scene to its intended place (Scene 5), certain advantages are immediately apparent. The eerie atmosphere of the scene with Woyzeck and Andres cutting sticks sets the tone for the whole play, and by placing the shaving scene after Woyzeck's first suspicions about Marie, the pompous moralising of the Captain becomes almost unbearably painful. It explains too Woyzeck's nervous energy and provides a cruel juxtaposition: Woyzeck earns a few groschen to give to his woman while she is giving herself to another man.

The Translation

This present translation is the first in English to take account of the latest research on Büchner. (Although it was equally available to Victor Price, the translator of the Oxford University Press volume *The Plays of Gerog Büchner*, his translation is based on the obsolete Bergemann edition.) That is not to say that our translator, John Mackendrick, has confined himself rigorously to the text as proposed in the above ordering of scenes. He has in fact taken up material from H1, H2 and H3 which Büchner probably did not intend to use, but each decision has been carefully weighed and does not proceed from ignorance.

This brings us to the problem of contamination, of including material from earlier drafts. At times this is unavoidable: for example, Scene 3 (the fairground) consists in H4 merely of a heading and one and a half blank pages. Büchner clearly intended to bring together his sketches in H1 and H2 to provide his final version, and a translator must do this too. At other times the decision to contaminate results from a number of considerations:

(i)   the play is, after all, unfinished with scenes in even the fair-copy left incomplete, and it is impossible to say with certainty that Büchner might not have had recourse to earlier material when submitting his final draft.

(ii) the play is very short and very compressed. While this does not matter to the reader, on stage it almost demands a certain extension either by the actors' use of pauses or by including dialogue from earlier drafts.

(iii) the earlier drafts, which Büchner seemingly rejected, still contain some staggeringly fine writing and some of the most memorable lines of the play. There is not so much good writing in the theatre that we can afford to lose it.

In practice, Mackendrick has taken up the following passages from the earlier drafts: H3: 1 (Doctor lecturing to his students), H2: 7 (Captain taunting Woyzeck in the street), H1: 8 (Woyzeck and Andres: 'What did he say?'). Any minor contaminations from earlier drafts are indicated by an asterisk in the following comparative table. The left-hand column shows the order of scenes in this translation, while the right-hand column indicates the corresponding scene (if any) in the table given above:

1.	Cutting sticks (*from H2)	1.
2.	Marie sees Drum-Major (*from H2)	2.
3.	Fairground (composed from H1 and H2)	3.
4.	Earrings.	4.
5.	Shaving Captain.	5.
6.	Doctor reproaches Woyzeck (*from H2)	8.
7.	Seduction.	6.
8.	Doctor lecturing students (H3).	–
9.	Doctor and Captain in street;	9.
	Captain taunts Woyzeck (H2)	–
10.	Woyzeck confronts Marie (*from H2)	7.
11.	Woyzeck leaves Andres to go to dance.	10.
12.	Woyzeck sees Marie at dance.	11.
13.	'Stab the she-wolf.'	12.
14.	Woyzeck tells Andres of voices.	13.

15.	Fight in the tavern.	14.
16.	Woyzeck and Andres: 'What did he say?' (H1)	—
17.	Woyzeck buys knife.	15.
18.	Marie reading Bible. (Fool omitted)	16.
19.	Woyzeck bequeathing belongings.	17.
20.	Grandmother's fable.	18.
21.	Woyzeck kills Marie.	19.
22.	Woyzeck returns to tavern.	21.
23.	Woyzeck returns to body, carries it into pond (own composition with material from H1)	—
	Passers-by hear cries.	20.
24.	Autopsy (own composition).	—
25.	Andres cutting sticks (own composition).	—

There are three points at which Mackendrick has departed from the presumed ordering of the original: first, to accommodate Scene 8 (Doctor lecturing students). Since Woyzeck here seems in a more advanced state of collapse ('I'm getting the shakes', 'everything's going dark on me again') than in his earlier meeting with the Doctor, the introduction of this scene at an appropriate point necessitates placing the 'Doctor reproaches Woyzeck' scene earlier in the play.

Secondly, by taking up the half scene in which the Captain taunts Woyzeck, it becomes much more meaningful to place the scene of Woyzeck's confrontation with Marie after the Captain's innuendoes rather than in its curiously crude placing immediately after Marie's seduction.

Finally, Mackendrick's own ending has led to the use of the scene, where the passers-by hear cries, to refer to Woyzeck's drowning rather than to the stabbing of Marie.

The ending of the play given by Mackendrick has a totally authentic ring and accords well with the evidence about Büchner's intentions, discussed above. It is a bold stroke to have Woyzeck return to wash Marie's body clean in the pond rather than to dispose of the knife, suggesting as it does a ritual act of purification from the sin she has committed. The next scene, the autopsy, is a completely free invention by Mackendrick, and he was unaware at the time that the possibility of an autopsy had been proposed in the very first edition of *Woyzeck* in 1879 and used as an ending many times since. Finally, the last scene with

Andres cutting his sticks recalls the opening scene, leaving the play open-ended yet providing a satisfying dramatic shape.

The two final scenes also succeed well in drawing together the social and existential strands of the piece. In the autopsy we see that Woyzeck, even in death, is exploited by being treated as a scientific specimen, and, even in death, is able to 'outwit' the Doctor by refusing to bleed. In the final scene we are reminded once more of the strange subterranean forces that play so important a role in the action.

Other changes that Mackendrick has made are as follows: in order to reduce the number of parts (given by Lehmann as 27 plus extras) to a manageable 13 (or 10 with doubling), he has excised the Fool in Scene 18 and given his lines in Scene 22 to the Grandmother. Similarly in Scene 20 Margaret and the Grandmother take the lines of the children; in Scene 22 Käthe's lines are given to Margaret; and the Journeymen speak the Landlord's lines in 22 and become the passers-by in 23. Small additions to the text, in each case to scenes which Büchner probably regarded as incomplete, are: from 'That's all woman' to the end of Scene 3 (the fairground); from 'Well, we must conclude' to the end of Scene 8 (Doctor lecturing students); and from beginning of Scene 17 (Woyzeck buying knife) to 'How much you got?' Apart from this, many of the stage-directions are Mackendrick's own, deriving from his own production of this translation at the Workshop Theatre of Leeds University in 1971, and in a few places the translation is deliberately free.

The problems of translating Büchner's language are considerable. His style is extremely compressed, creating poetry from everyday speech rhythms. As J.P. Stern writes: 'Words, everywhere in Büchner's work, are such strange, isolated objects: now like gaudy beads of poison, now like knives quivering in the target, now like scalpels dissecting living limbs, now again like gory wounds.'

The possibilities of the language are extended by dialect usage, by folk-song and folk-tale, by Bible and proverb, and by incremental repetition of key words and phrases. The language too is full of *Gestik*, that is, the quality of suggesting a gesture or action in the structuring of a phrase, so much so that stage-directions often seem redundant, since all is implied in the line. The modernity of the dialogue lies not only in the fact that this is almost certainly the first dialect play to have treated of a serious theme but also in the way language is used as a means of expression rather than communication. Characters frequently soliloquise together rather than conduct a dialogue, and in an extreme example like the first tavern scene (12) the songs, the drunken speeches and Woyzeck's monologue are all so disjointed that one could reverse their order or perform them simultaneously.

All these challenges have to be met by the translator, who also has to cope with the special qualities of the German language: the word 'blood' may express the meaning of the oft-repeated 'Blut', but it does not possess the sonorous quality of the full rounded vowel sound, and 'on and on' is a poor equivalent of 'immer zu' (Mackendrick reasonably expands it to 'on and on, round and round, for ever and ever'). Fortunately, John Mackendrick is ideally suited to the task. As author of *Lavender Blue*, which bears some similarities to *Woyzeck*, not least on account of the difficulties of finding an appropriate theatrical style, Mackendrick well understands how to combine poetry with realism and to unite social comment with dream-like fantasy. I think Büchner would have been well pleased.

Michael Patterson

Select Bibliography

For further reading the scholar of German is directed to the definitive Hamburger-Ausgabe of Büchner's writings, which contains all the drafts and major sources of Woyzeck:
Büchner, Georg. *Sämtliche Werke und Briefe.* Herausgegeben von
    Werner R. Lehmann. Vol. I. Christian Wegner Verlag,
    Hamburg, n.d. (1967), pp. 143-181, 337-431, 485-549.

For secondary literature he should consult the following:
Knapp, Gerhard P. *Georg Büchner.* Eine kritische Einführung in
    die Forschung. Athenäum Fischer Taschenbuch Verlag,
    Frankfurt am Main, 1975.
Schlick, Werner. *Das Georg Büchner-Schrifttum bis 1965.* Eine
    internationale Bibliographie. Georg Olms Verlagsbuch-
    handlung, Hildesheim, 1968.

The general reader may find the following useful:
Benn, Maurice B. *The Drama of Revolt.* A Critical Study of Georg
    Büchner. Cambridge University Press, London, 1976.
Hamburger, Michael. 'Georg Büchner', *Reason and Energy.*
    Studies in German Literature. Routledge & Kegan Paul,
    London, 1957, pp. 179-208.
Jacobs, Margaret. Introduction and notes to *Dantons Tod* and
    Woyzeck. 3rd edition. Manchester University Press,
    Manchester, 1971.
Knight, A.H.J. *Georg Büchner.* Basil Blackwell, Oxford, 1951.
Steiner, George. *The Death of Tragedy.* Faber & Faber, London,
    1961, pp. 270-281.
Stern, Joseph Peter. 'A World of Suffering: Georg Büchner'.
    Re-interpretations. Seven studies in nineteenth-century
    German literature. Thames & Hudson, London, 1964,
    pp. 78-155.

M.P.

Woyzeck

Characters

ANDRES, *soldier.*

WOYZECK, *soldier, with additional duties as batman.*

MARIE, *Woyzeck's common-law wife.*

MARGARET, *Marie's neighbour.*

DRUM-MAJOR, *specially privileged senior N.C.O. used as a mascot and for recruitment purposes. Chosen for physique, splendidly uniformed; excused normal duties.*

SHOWMAN*, *from the travelling fair.*

SERGEANT*, *associate of the Drum-Major.*

THE CAPTAIN, *for whom Woyzeck acts as batman.*

THE DOCTOR, *Regimental officer.*

1st JOURNEYMAN* } *artisans beyond apprenticeship who must*
2nd JOURNEYMAN* } *serve a period in another area before they become mastercraftsmen. A black uniform with headgear was worn.*

GRANDMOTHER, *very old. Blind.*

JEW*

*These parts may be doubled.

One

The woods. ANDRES *is splitting sticks and whistling the tune of his song.* WOYZECK *comes on to him.*

WOYZECK. The place is cursed, you know, Andres. You see that light strip on the grass there, where the toadstools're so thick? A head rolls down it every evening. There was a man picked it up once, he thought it was a hedgehog: three days and nights after, he was lying in his coffin.

(*Whispers.*) It was the Freemasons, Andres, I'm sure of it, the Freemasons.
— Quiet!

ANDRES (*sings*). A pair of hares were sitting there
            Nibbling the green, green grass . .

WOYZECK. Quiet.
Can you hear it, Andres? Can you hear it?
Something moving.

ANDRES. Nibbling the green, green grass
            Until the ground was bare.

WOYZECK. Moving behind me, beneath me —

He stamps on the ground.

Listen; it's hollow. It's all hollow under there.
— The Freemasons.

ANDRES. It's scary.

WOYZECK. So strange: still. 'Makes you hold your breath.
— Andres!

ANDRES.What?

WOYZECK. Say something!

He stares out across the landscape.

Andres! How bright! It's all glowing above the town, glowing.

A fire raging in the sky and clamour therebelow like trumpets. It's coming this way!

Drags ANDRES *into the bushes.*

Quick! Don't look behind you!

ANDRES.   . . .   Woyzeck? Can you still hear it?

WOYZECK. Silence, nothing but silence; as if the world w's dead.

ANDRES. The drums're going, listen. We've got to get back.

Two

MARIE *and* MARGARET *at* MARIE's *window as the retreat is being drummed.* MARIE *holds her child.*

MARIE. Hup, baby! Ta ra ra! — Hear it? — Here they come!

Precise and perfect, the DRUM-MAJOR *marches the length of the street.*

MARGARET. What a man, straight as a tree!

MARIE. And brave as a lion, I'll bet.

The DRUM-MAJOR *gives an eyes right salute.*
MARIE *acknowledges.*

MARGARET. Hey, that was a friendly eye you gave him neighbour! You don't treat every man to that.

MARIE (*sings*). Soldiers, they are handsome lads . .

MARGARET. Look at your eyes; still shining.

MARIE. So what? Take yours to the Jewman and let him polish them; you might be able to sell them for buttons if he c'n brighten them up.

MARGARET. Who're you to talk to me like that? Miss Motherhood! I'm an honest woman, I am, but you could see your way through seven pair of leather britches, you.

She goes out.

MARIE. Bitch.

Well, baby, let them have it their way. After all, you're only the child of a whore, unlucky thing; 'nd your wicked face just fills your mother's heart with joy.

> (*She sings*) What shall you do, my pretty maid?
> You've got a baby without a dad.
> Never you mind about me —
> All night long I'll sit and sing,
> 'Rockabye, rockabye, tiny thing,'
> Though nobody cares for me.

> Unsaddle your six white horses, do
> And give them fodder fresh and new —
> Oats they won't eat for you,
> Water won't drink for you,
> Nothing will do but wine, hop, hop,
> Nothing but pure, cold wine.

WOYZECK *comes to the window, knocks.*

— Who's there?
'That you, Franz? Come inside.

WOYZECK. 'Can't. 'Got to go to muster.

MARIE. Have you been cutting wood f'r the Captain?

WOYZECK. Yes.

MARIE. What's the matter, Franz? You look so wild.

WOYZECK. There was something there again, Marie, a lot of things.
— Isn't it written, 'And behold, there came forth a smoke from the land like the smoke of an oven'?

MARIE. Oh, man!

WOYZECK. It followed me all the way to town. — What does it mean?

MARIE. Franz!

WOYZECK. 'Got to go. — See you at the fair this ev'ning;
I've put something by.

> *He leaves.*

MARIE. That man! So haunted by everything. — He didn't even
stop to look at his child.
Thinking's wound his mind up like a watchspring, it'll break
one'v these days.
— Why're you so quiet, baby? Are you frightened?
It's so dark you could be going blind.   — No light.
The streetlamp usually shines in all the time. These shadows,
gathering like deadmen . .
It's horrible!

She hurries out with the child.

Three

*The fairground (at the edge of the woods). A voice sings over its
emptiness.*

> On earth is no abiding stay,
> All things living pass away —
> No-one, no-one says me nay.

MARIE *and* **WOYZECK** *come on.*

WOYZECK. An old man singing for a boy to dance to. Joy and
tribulation.

MARIE. People. When fools're wise it makes fools of the rest of
us.
Crazy old world, beautiful world!

A SHOWMAN comes out of his tent.

SHOWMAN. — Roll up, ladies and gentlemen! Come and see a
monkey walking upright like a man! He wears a coat and
trousers and carries a sword. Art improving on nature: our
monkey's a soldier. — Not that that's much. Lowest form of
animal life in fact.

No? Come and see the astronomical horse then. Admired by all the crowned heads 'v Europe. Tell you anything you like — how old you are, how many children you've got, what y'r illnesses are. Hurry now, the show's just opening! Hurry now, roll up — it's the commencemong of the commencemong!

WOYZECK. Want to go in?

MARIE. I don't mind. — Yes, let's, there must be all kinds of things.

They go into the tent as the SERGEANT *and* DRUM-MAJOR *enter the fairground.*

SERGEANT. Hold it. Look at that. — What a woman!

DRUM-MAJOR. Jesus, you could foal a cavalry regiment out of her. And breed drum-majors.

SERGEANT. Look 't the way she holds herself. That's what I call a body. All that meat to squeeze 'nd yet it moves as easy as a fish. Strange eyes —

DRUM-MAJOR. 'Make you think you're looking down a well, or a chimney. — Quick, it's starting! Get in.

They go inside and the SHOWMAN *takes their money.*

MARIE. — So bright!

WOYZECK. In the dark — black cats with fires in their eyes. 'Strange night.

SHOWMAN. Observe: the unique phenomenon of the astronomical horse.
— Show your paces now, show them y'r horse sense. Put humanity to shame.
Gentlemen, this animal you see before you with a tail and four hooves is a member of all the learned societies and, what's more, a professor at our university; where he teaches the students riding and kicking.
That's a straightforward matter of understanding, though.
— Now think inside-out. Show them what you can do when you use inside-out reasoning.

Is there an ass in this learned company?

The HORSE *shakes its head responsively.*

— See the effect of inside-out thinking? Done with equine-imity. Remarkable. This is no mute beast, I tell you; this is a person, a human being, an animalised human being — but still an animal.

The HORSE *defecates.*

That's it, put humanity to shame.   — This animal's still in a state of nature, you see, of plain, unvarnished nature! You ought to take a lesson from him. Ask your doctor, it's positively harmful to be any other way!
The message is: Man, be natural. You were fashioned out of dust, out of sand, out of mud — would you be anything more than dust, sand, mud?
Look here, how about this for the power of reason? The astronomical horse c'n calculate, but he can't count on his fingers. Why's that? Because he can't express himself, can't explain — in fact, he's a human being translated!
— Tell the gentlemen what time it is.
Has any of you ladies or gentlemen a watch? — A watch?

SERGEANT. A watch?

Produces one from his pocket magisterially.

There you are, sir.

MARIE. I must see this!

DRUM-MAJOR. That's all woman.

The HORSE *stamps its foot to tell the time.*

SHOWMAN. Eight o'clock! I ask you, is that not truly remarkable?!
— Ladies and gentlemen, this astonishing feat concludes the performance. Thanking you.

The DRUM-MAJOR *and* SERGEANT *watch* MARIE *out as she passes them, followed by* WOYZECK. *The* SHOWMAN *attends to his effects.*

SERGEANT. Give the man a hand, soldier.

> WOYZECK *helps the* SHOWMAN. *The* DRUM-MAJOR
> *follows* MARIE, *who walks off by the woods. Eventually, the*
> SERGEANT *lets* WOYZECK *go.*

WOYZECK. Marie?
Marie?

> *He runs out of the fairground. The* SERGEANT *and*
> SHOWMAN *exchange looks.*

Four

MARIE's room. She is tucking the baby into its crib.

MARIE. The man gives him an order and he has to go, just like
that.

> *She takes a piece of broken mirror from her blouse and*
> *examines the ear-rings she is wearing.*

Look how they catch the light. I wonder what they are?
What'd he say?
— Go to sleep, baby, shut your eyes tight.

> *She bends over towards the crib.*

Tighter. That's it. Now you keep still or else he'll come and
get you.
(*Sings.*) Polly, close the shutter tight,
       A gipsy lad will come tonight.
       He will take you by the hand
       And lead you off to gipsy land.
— They must be gold!
An old crack in the back wall of a corner to live in and a bit of
broken glass to see with, that's enough for the likes of us.
My mouth's as red as my lady's, though, for all her full-
length mirrors and rows of fine gentlemen kissing her hand.
An' I'm just another poor girl.
— Sshh, baby, close your eyes. (*She oscillates the fragment*)

Here comes the sandman, walking across the wall. Keep your eyes closed! If he looks in them you'll go blind.

WOYZECK *enters.* MARIE *starts and covers her ears.*

WOYZECK. What's that?

MARIE. Nothing.

WOYZECK. Under your fingers; it's shining.

MARIE. An ear-ring. I found it.

WOYZECK. I never found that kind of nothing. Two at once, too.

MARIE. So? What does that make me?

WOYZECK. You're alright, Marie.
'Kid's well away, look at him. 'Ll just move this arm so he doesn't get cramp.
Shiny drops, all over his forehead.   — Nothing but work under the sun; we even sweat in our sleep. The poor.
— 'Some more money, Marie. My pay and the extra from the Captain.

MARIE. God reward you, Franz.

WOYZECK.'Got to go. 'See you tonight. (*He goes out.*)

MARIE. Oh, I'm a bad bitch! I ought to cut my throat.
What sort of world d'you call this?
It's going to hell, all of it and us with it.

Five

The CAPTAIN *on his chair awaiting a shave.* WOYZECK *comes on to him.*

CAPTAIN. Slowly, Woyzeck, take it slowly. One thing *after* another one. You make me feel giddy.   — What am I supposed to do with the ten minutes you save rushing that way? What use are they to me? (WOYZECK *starts shaving him.*) Think about it, Woyzeck; you've got a good thirty years left.

Thirty years. That makes three hundred and sixty months —
and then there's days, hours, minutes! What're you going to do
with such a monstrous amount of time? Eh?
— Space it out a bit, Woyzeck.

WOYZECK. Yes, sir.

CAPTAIN. It makes me worried about the world, the thought of
eternity. It's some business, Woyzeck, some business!
Eternity . . is eternity . . is eternity — you can see that. But
it's also not eternity, it's a single moment, Woyzeck, yes, a
single moment. It's frightening, how the world turns round in
a day. What a waste of time! What does it amount to??
I can't stand to look at millwheels any more, they're so totally
depressing.

WOYZECK. Yes, sir.

CAPTAIN. You always look so wrought! A good citizen doesn't
look like that, Woyzeck, not a good citizen with a clear
conscience.
. . Say something, Woyzeck. — How's the weather today?

WOYZECK. Bad, sir, bad. Windy.

CAPTAIN. I'll say. There's a real wind out there, I can feel it.
'Makes my back prickle, as if a mouse w's running up and down
it.
. . (Slyly.) I should say it was a north-southerly.

WOYZECK. Yes, sir.

CAPTAIN. Ha ha ha! North-southerly. Ha ha ha!!   — God, but
the man's dense, horribly dense.
You're a good fellow, Woyzeck, but (Solemnly) you've no
morals.
Morals are . . well, observing morality, you understand.
That's the way of it. You've got a child without the church's
blessing, as our reverend padre calls it — without the church's
blessing; that's his expression.

WOYZECK. Sir, God the Father isn't going to worry if nobody
said amen at the poor worm's making. The Lord said,

'Suffer little children to come unto me'.

CAPTAIN. What do you mean? What an odd thing to say.
What you said, I mean, not what he said.
— You're confusing the issue.

WOYZECK. Being poor . .
D'you see, sir? Money, money! If you've no money   — .
Just you try getting one of our sort into the world in a moral
way; though we're flesh and blood as well. We never get much
luck, here or hereafter. If we went to heaven I expect they'd
put us to work on the thunder.

CAPTAIN. Woyzeck, you've no sense of virtue. You're not a
vituous man!
Flesh and blood?!
When I'm lying by my window, after it's been raining, and I
see a pair of white stockings twinkling down the street,
hop-skip . .
Dammit, Woyzeck, *I* feel desire then! I'm flesh and blood, too.
But my virtue, Woyzeck, my virtue! — So what do I do?
I keep saying to myself: You are a virtuous man . . (*Maudlin*)
a good man, a good man.

WOYZECK. Yes, sir. I don't think virtue's so strong in me, sir.
You see, people like us don't have any virtue, they only
have what's natural to them. But if I was a gentlemen and I
had a hat and a watch and a big coat and all the proper words,
I'd be virtuous alright. Must be a great thing, sir, virtue. Only
I'm just a poor man.

CAPTAIN. Well, Woyzeck, you're a good fellow, a good fellow.
But you think too much. You're wearing y'rself out, grinding
away 't things in there.
— You always look so wrought!
(*Stands.*) This discussion's upset me completely.
Get along now. (WOYZECK *removes the chair and his
    equipment.*)
And don't run! — Slowly. Nice and slowly down the street.

Six

The street. WOYZECK *against a wall, doing up his fly. The* DOCTOR *strides over and pulls him round roughly.*

DOCTOR. What d'you call this, Woyzeck? A man of your word, are you, eh? You? You?!

WOYZECK. What's the matter Doctor?

DOCTOR. I saw you, Woyzeck. You were pissing in the street, pissing like a dog down the wall — and I'm giving you two groschen a day, and board! It's bad, Woyzeck, bad. The whole world's going completely to the bad; completely.

WOYZECK. But, Doctor. When you get a call of nature —

DOCTOR. Call of nature! Call of *nature!* — Superstition, sheer, abominable superstition!
Nature!
Haven't I demonstrated conclusively that the musculus constrictor vesicae is subject to the will? — Nature!
Man is free, Woyzeck. Man is the ultimate expression of the individual urge to freedom. — Can't hold your water!
It's deceit, Woyzeck.

He shakes his head and paces, hands behind his back.

— Have you eaten your peas now, Woyzeck? You must eat nothing but peas, cruciferae, remember. We can start on the mutton next week. A revolution's taking place in science, I'm blowing the whole thing sky-high.
Uric acid 0.01, ammonium hydrochlorate, hyperoxide — Woyzeck, can't you have another piss? Go inside and try again!

WOYZECK. I can't, doctor.

DOCTOR *(Upset)*. Pissing against the wall, though! And I've a written undertaking, in your own handwriting! I saw it, saw it with these two eyes — I'd just stuck my nose out of the window and was letting the sunbeams play on it in order to observe the

phenomenon of the sneeze.   — Have you got me any frogs?
Or spawn? Fresh water polyps? No snakes? Vestillae?
Crystatelae?   — Be careful of the microscope, Woyzeck, I've
a germ's tooth under there. I'm going to blow the whole lot
sky-high!
No spiders' eggs? Toads'?
Oh, but pissing down the wall!   I *saw* you.
(Paces again in agitation.) No, Woyzeck, I shall not be angry.
Anger is unhealthy, unscientific. I am calm; completely calm.
My pulse is its usual sixty and I'm addressing you with the
utmost coolness. There's no reason for me to get angry with
you, you're only a man. If it'd been a question of one of the
newts dying, though —!   But really, Woyzeck, you shouldn't
have pissed down that wall —

WOYZECK. D'you see, Doctor? A man might have one sort of
    character, one sort of make-up — But nature's something
    again, you see: nature's a thing — *(Flicks his fingers to catch it.)*
    How c'n I say? For example —

DOCTOR. Woyzeck, you're philosophising again.

WOYZECK. Have you ever seen nature inside-out, Doctor? When
    the sun stands still at midday and it's 's if the world was going
    up in flames? That's when the terrible voice spoke to me.

DOCTOR. You've an aberration, Woyzeck.

WOYZECK. Yes. Nature, Doctor, when nature's out —

DOCTOR. What does that mean, 'when nature's out'?

WOYZECK. When nature's out, that's — when nature's *out*.
    When the world gets so dark you have to feel your way round
    it with your hands, till you think it's coming apart like a
    spider's web. When there's something there, yet there's
    nothing; and everything's dark but there's still this redness in
    the west like the glow of a huge furnace. When — *(Moves in
    starts as he tries to think it out.)*
    When —

DOCTOR. You're feeling your way with y'r feet like an insect,
    man!

WOYZECK. The toadstools, Doctor, it's all in the toadstools. Have you noticed how they grow in patterns on the ground? If only someb'dy could read them.

DOCTOR. Woyzeck, you've a beautiful aberratio mentalis partialis of the second order: fully formed, too. Beautiful. I shall give you a rise, Woyzeck! Second order: fixed idea with non-impairment of faculties.   — You're carrying on as usual, shaving the Captain?

WOYZECK. Yes, sir.

DOCTOR. Eating your peas?

WOYZECK. Just like you said, sir. The money helps my wife with the housekeeping.

DOCTOR. Performing your duties?

WOYZECK. Yes, sir.

DOCTOR. You're an interesting case, patient Woyzeck. It's a lovely idée fixe; certain to put you in the asylum. So bear up now, you're getting another groschen.
Give me your pulse, Woyzeck. Mm, yes.

WOYZECK. What do I do?

DOCTOR. Keep eating the peas and cleaning your rifle! You'll be getting another groschen soon.

Seven

MARIE's room. MARIE and the DRUM-MAJOR.

DRUM-MAJOR. Come on, Marie.

MARIE. Show me again, go round the room.

He reproduces his parade ground march.

The chest of an ox, with fur like a lion's mane. There's not another man like you. You make me proud to be a woman.

DRUM-MAJOR. You should see me Sundays with my plume and

gauntlets. That's really something. 'He's my idea of a soldier,' the prince always says, 'A real man.'

MARIE. Does he now?

(Goes up to him, teasing.) A real man. . ?

As he responds her mood changes and she moves away.

DRUM-MAJOR. And you're a real woman. Christ, I'm going to fill your belly full of drum-majors, sire a whole damn stable of them.   Come on.

Grabs her. She struggles, violently.

MARIE. Let me go!

DRUM-MAJOR. Wild, eh? Come on then, animal.

MARIE. Just you dare.

DRUM-MAJOR. 'Devil in you, isn't there? I can see it in your eyes.

MARIE *(Relaxes)*. What's it matter anyway? It's all one.

Eight

WOYZECK *comes in with a pair of steps, places them carefully, withdraws. The* DOCTOR *enters and ascends them to survey the audience, which he addresses as his assembled students.*

DOCTOR. Gentlemen, here I am aloft like David when he spied Bathsheba; but all I ever see is the boarding school girls' knickers hanging out to dry.   — Now, we come to the important question of the relation between subject and object. If we take one of those creatures in whom, gentlemen, the capacity of the divine for self-affirmation most clearly manifests itself and we examine its relation to space, the earth and the planetary universe. If, gentlemen, I take *(Producing it from his pocket)* this cat, and I throw it out of the window — what will be its instinctive behaviour relative to its centre of gravity?
— Woyzeck! — Woyzeck!!

He runs back in as the DOCTOR *throws the cat at him, which he catches.*

WOYZECK. Doctor, it's biting me!

DOCTOR. And look at you, nursing it like your grandmother. Fool.

WOYZECK. I'm getting the shakes, Doctor.

DOCTOR *(Pleased, descending)*. Is that so? How interesting. How very, very interesting.
And what's this, a new species of animal louse? 'Fine one, too.

Takes out a magnifying glass to mock-examine the cat.

WOYZECK. You're frightening it. *(Takes the cat out.)*

DOCTOR. Animals have no scientific instincts. — Therefore, I shall use another demonstration subject.

Clicks his fingers. WOYZECK *returns.*

Observe, gentlemen. For three months this man has eaten nothing but peas. Note the effect, it's clearly apparent.
The pulse is irregular, singularly. And the eyes: note the peculiarity of the eyes.

WOYZECK. Doctor — everything's going dark on me again.

Teeters, almost falling onto the steps.

DOCTOR. Cheer up, Woyzeck. Just a few more days and it'll all be over.

He prods at glands and points of the thorax.

The effect is palpable, gentlemen, palpable.
— Just wiggle your ears for the young gentlemen while we're at it, Woyzeck.
I meant to show you this before. He uses the two muscles quite independently.   — Go on then.

WOYZECK *(embarrassed)*. Oh, Doctor —

DOCTOR. Do I have to wiggle them for you, you brute?! Are you going to behave like the cat? — There you are, gentlemen, another case of progressive donkeyfication resulting from

female upbringing and the use of the German language!
You're losing your hair. Has your mother been pulling it
out for mementos?
Ah, no, it's the peas, gentlemen, the peas.
Well, we must conclude. Thank you all. Woyzeck, when you've
taken those back the Captain wants to see you.

WOYZECK. Yes, sir.

The DOCTOR *goes out,* WOYZECK *following with the steps.*

Nine

The street. The DOCTOR *walks briskly down it with the*
CAPTAIN *puffing after him.*

CAPTAIN. Doctor. Just a minute, Doctor! You shouldn't go
so fast, you know. The only thing you'll catch up with
rushing like that's y'r last day. A good man with a clear
conscience doesn't hurry that way. A good man. *(Snorts,
breathes heavily to regain himself.)*

The DOCTOR *tries to move away but the* CAPTAIN *has him
by his coat.*

Allow me the privilege of saving a human life, Doctor.

DOCTOR *(Agitating his arm)*. I'm in a hurry, Captain. A hurry!

CAPTAIN. My dear ghoul, you'll wear your legs down to the
pavement. Stop trying to take off on your stick.

DOCTOR. I'll tell you something — your wife will be dead inside
four weeks. Total collapse occasioned by complications in the
seventh month. I've had twenty identical cases: they all died.
Inside four weeks — you'd better start getting used to the idea.

CAPTAIN. Please, Doctor, I get so depressed; it's making me
imagine things. I can't look at my empty coat hung up on the
wall without bursting into tears.

DOCTOR. Hm. — Puffy, fat; thick neck. Apoplectic type.
Yes, Captain, that'll be the way of it. You're a certainty for

apoplectic seizure of the brain. . . Of course, you might only
be affected down one side, hemi-paresis, then you'd still be
able to move the unparalysed half of your body. Or
alternatively you might be even luckier and have simply local
cerebral paralysis, in which case you'd become a sort of human
potato.

Yes, that's the outlook for you in the next month. Though
there's also the possibility that you could become a really
interesting case by having just one half of your tongue paralysed.
Now if that happens I'll be able to do experiments on it that
will make you go down in medical history.

CAPTAIN. Don't frighten me like that, Doctor. People have been
known to die of fright, you know, of sheer bloody fright.

— I can see the mourners already, getting the lemons out'v
their pockets to make them cry. Still, they'll say, 'He was a
good man; a good man.' — Oh, you damned old coffin nail!

DOCTOR. Ha. Do you see this? *(Holds up his hat.)*
This, my dear squarebasher, is an empty headpiece.

CAPTAIN. And this *(Displays one of his buttons)*, my dear ghoul,
is a bonehead. Ha ha ha! — No offence, mind. I'm a virtuous
man, but I can give as good as I get when I feel like it, Doctor.
Ha ha ha! When I feel like it —

WOYZECK *comes down the street trying to avoid notice.*

— Hey! Woyzeck!
Where're you dashing off to? Just wait there a minute, Woyzeck.
You go through the world like an open razor. You'll be giving
someone a nasty cut one of these days. Have you got to
shave a regiment of eunuchs on pain of death if you miss one
hair or something? Eh?

On the subject of hairs, that puts me in mind of the saying —
You know, Woyzeck —

DOCTOR. Pliny states: troops are to be discouraged from
wearing facial hair.

CAPTAIN. The one about finding a hair from someone else's
beard in your soup. — You take my meaning?

Or perhaps we should say in this case, from someone else's
moustache — a sapper's, or a sergeant's, or, maybe, a drum-
major's?
Eh, Woyzeck?
But then, your wife's a good woman, isn't she? Not like some.

WOYZECK. Yes, sir. What do you mean, sir?

CAPTAIN. Look at the man's face!
You might not find that hair in your soup, but if you popped
round the corner you could just find it sticking to a certain pair
of lips. A certain pair of lips, Woyzeck.
Ah yes, I've known love in my time, too.
— Good God, you've turned to chalk, man; you're stone white!

WOYZECK. Captain, I'm a poor man — I've nothing but her in
the world. Please don't make jokes, sir.

CAPTAIN. Make jokes? Me, make jokes with you?!

DOCTOR. Pulse, Woyzeck, pulse!
Short, skipping, violent, irregular.

WOYZECK. The earth's hotter th'n hell .. and I'm cold.
Ice. Ice.
Hell must be cold, I'm sure.   — It's not possible!
Slut! Slut!!   — Not possible.

CAPTAIN. What are you doing, staring at me like that? Do you
want a bullet in the brain, man?!   Your eyes're like knives.
— I'm only doing you a favour, it's for your own good.
Because you're not a bad fellow, Woyzeck, not such a bad
fellow.

DOCTOR. Facial muscles taut, rigid; occasional twitches.
Manner tense, hyperexcited.

WOYZECK. I'm off. Anything can be possible.   — The slut!
Anything at all.
— 'Fine day, Captain, isn't it? With a fine grey, stone sky.
You c'd just hammer a peg in it and hang yourself.
All because of the little pause between 'Yes' and 'Yes' again —
and 'No'.

Yes and No, Captain.   — Is the No to blame for the Yes, or
the Yes for the No?
I sh'll have to think about that.

Moves away, step by step at first then increasingly quickly.

DOCTOR. Unique, unique! *(Runs after him.)*
Woyzeck! Another rise, Woyzeck!

CAPTAIN. People, they make me dizzy. — Look at them. One
sparking and veering while the other reaches after him like a
spider's shadow.
Thunder following lightning. — Grotesque, grotesque!
I don't like such things. A good man takes care of himself,
takes care of his life; he isn't foolhardy. No, foolhardiness is
for scoundrels, for dogs!
I'm not like that.

Ten

MARIE's *room.* WOYZECK *is staring at her with mad intensity.*

WOYZECK. I can't see anything. Can't see anything.
It should show! You should be able to see it, get hold of it
with y'r hands!

MARIE. Franz? What's the matter? You're raving.

WOYZECK. What a fine street — you could wear your feet to
stumps on it! It's good to stand in the street . .   Even better
when there's company.

MARIE. Company?

WOYZECK. Lots'v people can walk down a street, can't they?
And you can talk to them, to whoever you choose. And it's
nothing to do with me!
Did he stand here? — Then close to you? So?
Oh, I wish I'd been him.

MARIE. Him? — What're you talking about? I can't stop people
coming down the street or make them wear muzzles, can I?

WOYZECK. And your lips're so beautiful — it's a shame you couldn't leave them at home.
But that would've brought the wasps in, I suppose.

MARIE. Well which wasp's bitten you then? You're like the cow th't the hornets stung.

WOYZECK. Such a sin. Such a great, gleaming, fat one — it reeks! You'd think the stink of it would bring the angels tumbling out of heaven.
Your mouth's so red, Marie. Why're there no blisters on it?
Why're you so beautiful, Marie? As beautiful as sin.
Can mortal sin be beautiful?

MARIE. You're delirious.

WOYZECK. Did he stand here?! So?! Did he!?!

MARIE. Days're long and the world's old. A lot of people c'n stand in the same place, one after another.

WOYZECK. I can see him!!

MARIE. You c'n see lots'v things, if you've eyes 'nd the sun shining 'nd you're not blind.

WOYZECK. (*Goes to strike her*) — Slut!!

MARIE. Don't touch me, Franz!
Put a knife in my guts if you want but not your hand on mine.
My own father didn't dare do that when I was ten years old.
He couldn't while I looked him in the face, and you won't now.

WOYZECK. Whore!
No, it would have to show. — Everyone's an abyss. You get dizzy if you look down.
Just suppose! — She walks like any innocent.
Oh, innocence, there's a stain on your robe.
Am I sure? Sure? — Who's ever sure? (*Goes out.*)

Eleven

The guardroom. ANDRES *is cleaning his boots and singing.*
WOYZECK *is sitting down.*

ANDRES. The landlord has a pretty wife,
      Sits in the garden day and night;
      She sits in the garden waiting —

WOYZECK. Andres!

ANDRES. What now?

WOYZECK. A fine evening out.

ANDRES. Yeh, Sunday weather alright.
There's some music later, over the heath. The women've gone
up there already. 'Be some sweat shed, you can bet.

WOYZECK. Dancing, Andres. They'll be dancing!

ANDRES. At The Horse 'nd The Star, that's right.

WOYZECK. Dancing, dancing!

ANDRES. Why not?
(*Sings.*) She sits in the garden waiting —
Until the village clock strikes twelve
And the solidier-boys come marching.

WOYZECK. Andres — I can't get any rest from it.

ANDRES. More fool you.

WOYZECK. 'Got to get out. Everything spins round. — Dancing,
dancing!
Her hands'll be hot.   — Oh, damn her, Andres, damn her!

ANDRES. What's the matter with you?

WOYZECK. 'Got to go. 'See for myself.

ANDRES. Why make trouble? Over one like that.

WOYZECK. 'Got to get out. It's stifling. (*Goes.*)

Twelve

The tavern. Redness, heat. A crowd including MARGARET, *two*
JOURNEYMEN *and the old* GRANDMOTHER, *who is blind
with cataracts. The* FIRST JOURNEYMAN *is singing.*

1st JOURNEYMAN. I've got a shirt on, but it isn't mine:
My soul is stinking with brandy wine —

2nd JOURNEYMAN. Let me punch a hole in your face, brother,
for friendship's sake. Come on, I'm going to punch a hole in
your face. — I'm twice the man he is any day!
'Smash every flea on y'r body to bits.

1st JOURNEYMAN. My soul *is*, my soul is stinking with brandy
wine.
Even money rots.   — My little forget-me-not; why is the
world so beautiful? I could weep a sea of buckets at the sad-
ness of it, brother.   — I wish our noses w're both bottles;
we could empty them down one another's throats.

Some of the others begin to clap and the two JOURNEYMEN
dance peasant fashion as everyone sings.

ALL. There were two hunters from the Rhine
Rode through the woods in clothes so fine.
Tally-ho! Tally-ho! Merrily we'll go,
Roaming together the wild woods free —
A hunter's life is the life for me!

WOYZECK *enters.*

A hunter's life is the life for me!

MARIE *and the* DRUM-MAJOR *appear outside, dancing.*

WOYZECK. Him. Her
Hell. — Hell, hell!

They spin a long, elaborate revolve.

MARIE. On and on —

DRUM-MAJOR. Round and round —

MARIE. For ever and ever —
On and on and on . .

They dance away. WOYZECK *is stricken, the crowd silent as they watch.*

WOYZECK. On and on. On and on and on! (*Staggers, lurching towards the spectators.*)
For ever! (*Beats his fist on his palm.*)
Turn, turn. Go on turning, dancing! — Why don't you blow the sun out, God? Let everything fall over itself in lewdness. Flesh, filth, man, woman, human, animal. — They all do it in the open day, do it on the back of a hand like flies.
Slut!!   — She's hot, hot! (*Staggers again.*)

He falls down, catches onto a bench.

— Feeling his way round her, round her body.
Him. He's got her . . Like I had her at the beginning.

He collapses. Everyone talks at once. The FIRST JOURNEY-MAN *goes to where* WOYZECK'S *lying and turns to still them.*

1st JOURNEYMAN. Brethren — think now upon The Wanderer, who stands poised beside the stream of time and communes with himself, receiving the wisdom of God and saying, 'Wherefore is man?' And again, 'Wherefore is man?'
Verily, verily I say to you, how should the farmer, the cooper, the doctor, the shoemaker live if God had not created man? How should the tailor ply his trade, if God had not implanted shame in the human breast? Or the soldier his, if man had not been equipped with the need for self-destruction?
Therefore, be not afraid . .
Yes, it's all very fine, very wonderful, but the earth's vain. Even money rots.
So, in conclusion, beloved — let's piss on the crucifix and a Jew will die!

WOYZECK *comes to and runs out.*

Thirteen

The woods beyond.

WOYZECK. On and on! For ever! On, on, on!
Stop the music. — Shh.
(*Throws himself down.*) What's that? — What's that you say?
What're you saying?
. . Stab. . . Stab the she-wolf, dead.
Shall I?
Must I?
— Is it there, too? In the wind even.

(*Stands up.*) It's all round me. Everywhere. Round, round,
on and on and on . . .

Stab her. Dead, dead — dead!! (*Runs out.*)

Fourteen

The guardroom. ANDRES *asleep in a blanket.* WOYZECK *comes
in, shakes him.*

WOYZECK. Andres, Andres! — I can't sleep. Everything starts
spinning when I shut my eyes and I hear the fiddles — on and
on, round and round. Then it says it again, out of the wall.
Can you hear it?

ANDRES.(*Mumbles*) Yes, yes; let th'm dance.
(*Turns over.*) 'Man gets tired. God save us. Amen.

WOYZECK. Always the same — stab, stab!
Between my eyes. Like a knife.

ANDRES.Get to bed, y'fool.
(*Goes back to sleep.* WOYZECK *goes out.*)

Fifteen

The tavern, late. The DRUM-MAJOR *is seated alone at one side. Others grouped carefully away from him.* WOYZECK.

DRUM-MAJOR. I'm a man! (*Pounds his chest*).
A man! D'you hear? — Who's looking f'r a fight? If y're not
's pissed 's creeping Jesus keep away from me. I'll ram y'r nose
up your arse!
(*To* WOYZECK.) Hey, you, drink up. Everyone has to drink.
drink. I wish the world w's made'v schnapps, me, schnapps —
I said, everyone has to drink. You: drink.
WOYZECK *whistles*
You little shit.
I'll rip the tongue from y'r throat and strangle you with it.

Throws himself on WOYZECK, *who takes a bad beating in the ensuing fight. It ends with him on the ground.*

Bastard; rat turd. I'm going to knock the breath out'v you
alright. You won't have enough f'r an old woman's fart.

Jumps on WOYZECK'S *back with his knees.*

— Now try and whistle, shit. You c'n whistle y'rself sky-blue
f'r all I care.
(*Sings*) Oh — brandy is the drink for me;
Brandy gives a man spunk!

Goes for more drink. The crowd feel free to talk.

2nd JOURNEYMAN. He's had his bellyful.

MARGARET. Look, he's bleeding.

WOYZECK *starts to rise, falls again.*

WOYZECK. One thing after another.

Sixteen

Morning, the guardroom. ANDRES *with a towel.* WOYZECK
comes in to him.

WOYZECK. Was he in the washroom? Did he say anything?

ANDRES. (*Dries his face*) He w's with his mates.

WOYZECK. What'd he say? What'd he *say*?

ANDRES. What's the difference?
    What d'you want him to say — a red-hot piece, fantastic, h'r
    inside's like running butter?

WOYZECK. (*cold*) So that's what he said.
    What was I dreaming about last night? A knife, was it?
    Stupid things, dreams.

    Gathers his kit up.

ANDRES. Where're you off to?

WOYZECK. 'Fetch my officer's wine.
    — But you know, Andres, there was no-one like her.

ANDRES. Who?

WOYZECK. 'Doesn't matter.   —'See you.

    He goes out.

Seventeen

The JEW *in his shop.* WOYZECK *enters.*

WOYZECK. Any guns?

JEW. Maybe.

WOYZECK. How much?

JEW. Four crowns, five crowns. How much you got?

WOYZECK. 'S too dear.

JEW. You buy, you don't buy. Which?

WOYZECK. How much for a knife?

JEW. This one?
    Lovely straight, this one. — You want to cut your throat with
    it? So, what's that? I give you cheap — same price as anyone

else. Cheap you can have your death; not for nothing.
So, what's that? You get death economical.

WOYZECK. (*Feels*) It'll cut more th'n bread.

JEW. Two groschen.

WOYZECK. Take it.

Pushes the money into his hand and goes.

JEW. Take it!
Just like that: as if it was nothing. — And it's money, all of it
money.
Dog!

Eighteen

MARIE'S *room. The child is in its crib*, MARIE *knelt nearby with an
an open Bible.*

MARIE. '. . Neither was guile found in his mouth.'

Looks across at the crucifix.

Don't look at me, Lord.

She turns to another page.

'And the scribes and the pharisees brought unto him a woman
taken in adultery, and set her in the midst . . And Jesus said
unto her, Neither do I condemn thee. Go, and sin no more.'

Tries to hold her hands together in prayer.

I can't. — Can't.
Dear God, don't take everything, at least let me pray.

The child stirs and she comforts him.

And Franz doesn't come. Yesterday, today. 'Still doesn't
come.
— It gets so hot!

Goes to the window and opens it, comes back to the Bible.

She picks it up and reads where she's standing.

'. . And she stood at his feet behind him weeping, and began to wash his feet with tears and did wipe them with the hairs of her head, and kissed his feet and anointed them with an ointment.'

Strikes herself on the breast.

Dead; all dead!   — Oh my Lord, my Lord!
If only I could anoint your feet.

Nineteen

The guardroom. WOYZECK *is going through his kitbag,* ANDRES *watching.*

WOYZECK. This waistcoat's not standard issue, Andres. You might be able to use it for something.
The cross belongs to my sister, so does the ring. I've got a holy picture somewhere too, a pair of twined hearts — my mother used to keep it in her bible. There's a motto: Christ, as your heart was red and wounded, so let mine be cleft and sundered. She's no feeling left, my mother, only when the sun shines on h'r hands.
— Doesn't matter.

ANDRES. 'Course.

WOYZECK. (*Pulls out a sheet of paper*)'Friedrich Johann Franz Woyzeck. Rifleman. Second Fusiliers Regiment, Second Battalion, Fourth Company. Born on the Feast of The Annunication —'
I'm thirty years old. Thirty years, seven months and twelve days.

ANDRES. You ought to report sick, Franz, you're not right. Have a schnapps with powder in it to kill the fever.

WOYZECK. That's it, Andres.
When the carpenter collects his shavings for the box, no-one knows whose head'll lie on them.

Twenty

The street. MARIE *and* MARGARET *standing by the* GRAND-MOTHER, *seated.*

MARGARET. (*Sings*) At Candlemas the sun shines bright,
             The corn stands up to drink the light
             And everywhere, the meadows through,
             The folk come dancing two by two.
             Oh pipers put your best foot first,
             Fiddlers fiddle until you burst
             And kick your red legs in the air —

GRANDMOTHER. I don't like that one.

MARGARET. What d'you want then?

GRANDMOTHER. You sing, Marie.

MARIE. No.

MARGARET. Why not?

MARIE. Because.

MARGARET. Because what?

MARIE. Just because.

MARGARET. All right, Grandma 'll tell us a story.

GRANDMOTHER. Sit, sit.
    Once upon a time there was a poor little boy who had no
    father and mother; everything was dead and there was no-one
    left in the whole world. Everthing was quite dead, so he went
    off, whimpering. All day and all night. And since there was
    no-one left on earth he decided to go up to heaven where the
    moon shone down so kind. But when he got to the moon it
    was a lump of rotten wood. Then he went to the sun, but
    when he got there it was a withered-up sunflower. And when
    he got to the stars they were little spangled midges stuck there,
    like the ones shrikes stick on blackthorns. So he went back to
    the earth, but the earth was an overturned pot. He was
    completely alone, and he sat down and cried. He's sitting
    there still, all alone.

WOYZECK *comes into the street.*

WOYZECK. Marie!

MARIE. (*Starts*) What is it?

WOYZECK. We've to go, Marie, it's time.

MARIE. Go where?

WOYZECK. Does it matter?

They go down the street.

Twenty one

The woods. WOYZECK *and* MARIE *come through them slowly.*

MARIE. The town's that way. It's dark.

WOYZECK. Stay a bit. Here, sit down.

MARIE. I've got to get back.

WOYZECK. You won't get sore feet from walking. I'll save you that.

MARIE. What're you on about?

WOYZECK. D'you know how long it's been, Marie?

MARIE. Two years this Whitsun.

WOYZECK. D'you know how long it's going to be?

MARIE. I've got to go, there's supper to get.

WOYZECK. Are you cold, Marie?
'Nd yet you're warm! — And you've hot lips, hot breath. Hot, hot whore's breath! I'd give heav'n to kiss them again, though.
When we're really cold, then we don't feel the weather any more. You won't feel the damp in the morning.

MARIE. What's that you say?

WOYZECK. Nothing.

A silence.

MARIE.   The moon's up. 'All red.

WOYZECK.   Like blood on iron.

MARIE. What d'you mean? — Franz, you're so pale.

He draws the knife.

No, Franz!
Merciful God. Help! Help!

He stabs her.

WOYZECK.   There! There! There!
Why don't you die?   — Die, die!!
— Ha, still moving? Even now; even now?

He holds the head back and cuts her throat.

Still moving?

Lets the body fall.

Now are you dead? Now?
Dead. Dead. Dead.

He moves away backwards from the body, then turns and runs.

Twenty two

The tavern. The same people, dancing. WOYZECK *bursts in.*

WOYZECK.   Dance! Dance! Everyone dance!   — Sweat, stink,
round and round!
He'll come for you all in the end.

He joins in the dance and sings.

> My daughter, oh my daughter,
> What were you thinking of —
> Hanging round grooms and coachmen
> And giving them your love?

— So, Margaret, sit down. — I'm hot, hot!
That's the way it is, the devil takes one and lets the other go.
You're hot, Margaret. Why's that? You'll be cold, too. Yes,

cold.
You want to be careful!
— Why don't you sing something?

MARGARET. (*Sings*) To the South Land I'll not go,
      I will not wear long dresses, no;
      For dresses long and pointed shoes
      A serving-girl must never choose.

WOYZECK. No. No shoes. You c'n get to hell without shoes.

MARGARET. (*Sings*) Oh no, my love, the girl made moan —
Keep your money and sleep alone.

WOYZECK. That's right. I wouldn't want to get myself all
bloody.

MARGARET. What's that then? On your hand!

WOYZECK. Where?

MARGARET. (*Backs away*) You're all red! — With blood!

WOYZECK. With blood?
With blood?

The crowd has gathered.

1st JOURNEYMAN. Ai — blood!

WOYZECK. 'Must have cut myself, cut my hand.

2nd JOURNEYMAN. How'd it get on your elbow then?

WOYZECK. When I wiped it off.

2nd JOURNEYMAN. Wipe that hand on that elbow? You'd
have t'be a genius.

GRANDMOTHER. Fee fie fo fum. I smell the blood of a dead
wo-man.

WOYZECK. What d'you want, dammit? What's going on? Give
me some room, or else —
Hell, d'you think I've done someone in? 'Think I'm a
murderer? What're you staring at? Take a look at yourselves!

Rushes through them.

Give me room! Room!

He runs away.

Twenty three

The woods. MARIE'S *body where it fell.* WOYZECK *comes through the shadows.*

WOYZECK. Getting closer. Closer
This is a strange place. Weird. — What's that?
Something moving. — Shh. Just there.
— Marie?

He moves and stumbles onto the body. It shows bloody in the light.

Aah!
Marie.
— So still. — Everything so still.

He kneels on one knee by the body. Pulls the trunk up onto him resting her back on his knee, holding her like a child.

Why're you so pale, Marie?
What's that red thing round your neck? Is it a necklace?
Who gave you a necklace to commit sins with him?
Oh, you were black with them, black.
Have I made you white again?
Why's your hair so wild, Marie? — Didn't you comb it today?
So, I'll tidy it for you. You have to look your best, there'll be people to meet.
What're all these marks? Look. Here, here. Like bloodstains.
How did you get them? Have you been fighting, Marie?

Starts to lift the body.

You have to get up now, then I can wash you.
It's not far. Up.

Stands upright with the body held in front of him.

There's water here, to wash you. To wash everything away, then you'll be clean. — Come to the water.

Drags her down to the pool side.

D'you see the moon, Marie? There's even blood on the moon. But you'll be clean.
Take a step. Then another.
And another.
Another.
— Water, Marie. All the water in the world to wash you.
Water —

They disappear into the pool. Silence.

The two JOURNEYMEN *come by the wood carefully, halt.*

2nd JOURNEYMAN.   What's the matter?

1st JOURNEYMAN.   Can't you hear it? — There.

2nd JOURNEYMAN.   Ei! What a sound!

1st JOURNEYMAN.   'The water, calling. No-one's been drowned for a long time. It's bad luck to hear it. Come on!

2nd JOURNEYMAN.   There! Again. Like a death-cry.

1st JOURNEYMAN.   Uncanny . .
Fog creeping in — Everywhere grey. Beetles whirring like cracked bells.
— Come on!

Twenty four

The morgue. MARIE *and* WOYZECK'S *corpses under sheets. The* DOCTOR *comes in with his instrument case. Looks at them, then lifts the sheet on* MARIE. *He indents the body with his finger at various points and sniffs it.*

DOCTOR. Hmm.
Little decomposition. Minor contusions.

Multiple laceration and perforation to a point — some
millimetres forward of the spine. No vertebral displacement.
One right side tendon intact.
General pallor, modified rigor; abdominal distension.
Consistent with a prolonged immersion.

Takes out a large knife and incises the muscle wall.

Confirmed by comparative absence of blood, fluid or static.

*Kneels up on the slab and takes his saw from the case. Uses it
to cut briskly through the rib cage. Lays down the saw, takes
up his knife and incises again deeply.*

Non-evidence of water in the lung. Indicative of post-mortem
immersion.
'Routine case. — Death by asphyxiation, occasioned by
transverse passage of an unknown instrument across the
trachea, probably a knife.
Yes: routine, routine.

*Climbs down, imperfectly replacing the sheet on her. Crosses
to* WOYZECK'S *body with his case, exposes the head.*

Ah, Woyzeck.
What a waste! Just when you were really becoming interesting.
No consideration. — If you'd only stopped to think!
You could have been in the asylum now, Woyzeck, visited by
all the foremost medical practitioners.
The trouble I took with you. — Waste, waste.

He pulls the sheet back fully.

A very poor cadaver.
No exceptional disfigurement; no marks of violence. — Normal
decomposition consistent with immersion in water.
Hmm —

Punctures the body casually with his knife.

Presence of same commensurate with death by drowning.
A poor ending, Woyzeck.

The CAPTAIN *enters portentously.*

CAPTAIN. A bad business, Doctor.
These people — Their lives —
Messy.

DOCTOR. Putrefaction is the process whereby chemical fats
comprising the tissue are rendered to their constituent
elements. A disagreeable odour may be discerned.

CAPTAIN. I knew he'd come to a bad end. — Woyzeck, I said,
this dashing about'll do you no good at all. You're only
running toward the grave.
And now he's got there, ahead of time.
It's a sad world, Doctor, going on the way it does for ever
without stopping. — How can it have time to think?!

DOCTOR. Absence of scientific method, Captain! Proceed
empirically. By the use of the empirical faculty I have been
able to establish that this woman had her throat cut and this
man died by drowning.

CAPTAIN. Oh, marvellous — marvellous! To work that out from
them being found in the lake and her with her head hanging
off!

DOCTOR. Deduction, deduction.
This corpse has no water in the lung and no blood. — This
corpse has water in the lung and blood in a condition of stasis.
Observe.

He incises WOYZECK'S *body.*

What's this? Where's the blood? — What have you done with
your blood, Woyzeck?

CAPTAIN. Ha ha! Deduction, my dear ghoul — he's lost it.

DOCTOR. I shall report this. It's an affront to medicine.

Gathers up his instruments and packs them quickly.

CAPTAIN. Don't rush off, Doctor. Look here, look what comes
of it. — I haven't told you my symptoms yet. This business's
upset me dreadfully, I get indigestion —

DOCTOR. (*Pauses*) Where's the blood, Woyzeck? What's happened
to the blood?

Goes out urgently.

CAPTAIN. (*Follows*) Doctor! Wait!

Twenty Five

The woods, ground mist. ANDRES, kneeling, splits sticks. A voice whistles the first line of 'I had a little nut tree', making him look round. He recommences chopping.

ANDRES. Wha — ?

Feels among the sticks, looks at his fingers.

'Must've cut myself. Cut my hand.

The second line is whistled, closer. ANDRES hardly hears. He examines his fingers.

Eh?

Scrabbles at the sticks. The GRANDMOTHER appears behind him in a cloak and hood.

Where — ?

He picks the sticks up tentatively: their undersides are running with gore. It drips. ANDRES drops them, backs away.

It's coming out 'the ground. — Coming out 'the ground!

The GRANDMOTHER laughs. He runs off.

She walks forward as the mist thickens round her and is then lit red, reflecting on her cataracts. She looks round the wood. The voice whistles 'I had a little nut tree' again, but moving further and further away this time.

The GRANDMOTHER nods and moves off slowly as the mist thickens to opacity.

Translator's Note

The fairy tale is quite deserted,
Its meres are frozen, roads broken,
Gates and purposes rotted away.
Frost spines the thistle's ruff
In the place where the cornfield was;
All the fieldmice have been harvested.

The castle walls fell into the moat,
The courtyard turned into mud;
Armorial banners, screaming maids
And the rest of the palace debris
Floated a while in one or the other
Then sunk. Mud and moat froze over them.

Only the solitary iron tower survives,
Built to circle the mad prince's life
With silence, rusting round the instant
That split it as the scream did his throat,
His chains and the guard's transfixed amazement
At red bubbles blinking on his borrowed penknife.

In the storyteller's mind — unhinged
Like a dislocated limb — the moment spins.